Bob der Baumeister

Bildwörterbuch

Deutsch – Englisch

XENOS

ISBN 3-8212-3025-8

www.bobthebuilder.com

Verantwortlich für diese Ausgabe:
© Xenos Verlagsgesellschaft mbH
Am Hehsel 40, 22339 Hamburg
Text: Antje Bones
Satz, Litho & Layout: D-to-B, Hamburg
Printed in Slovakia

Inhalt – content

Bob und Wendy – Bob and Wendy

Hallo, ich bin Bob der Baumeister.
Hello, I'm Bob the Builder.

Bob und Wendy – Bob and Wendy

Hallo! Ich heiße Wendy.
Hello! My name is Wendy.

Bob und Wendy – Bob and Wendy

Bob trifft Wendy im Büro. **Bob meets Wendy in the office.**
Sie besprechen, welche Arbeiten sie heute zu erledigen haben.
They are discussing which jobs they have to do today.

Bob und Wendy – Bob and Wendy

Das Team – The Team

Hallo, mein Name ist Mixi!
Hello, my name is Mixi!

Was machen wir heute, Bob?
What are we going to do today, Bob?

Ich kann's mischen!
I can mix it!

Ich bin Heppo.
Ich kann's hochheben!
I am Heppo. I can lift it!

Etwas zu bauen, macht so viel Spaß!
Building things is so much fun!

Das Team – The Team

Das Team – The Team

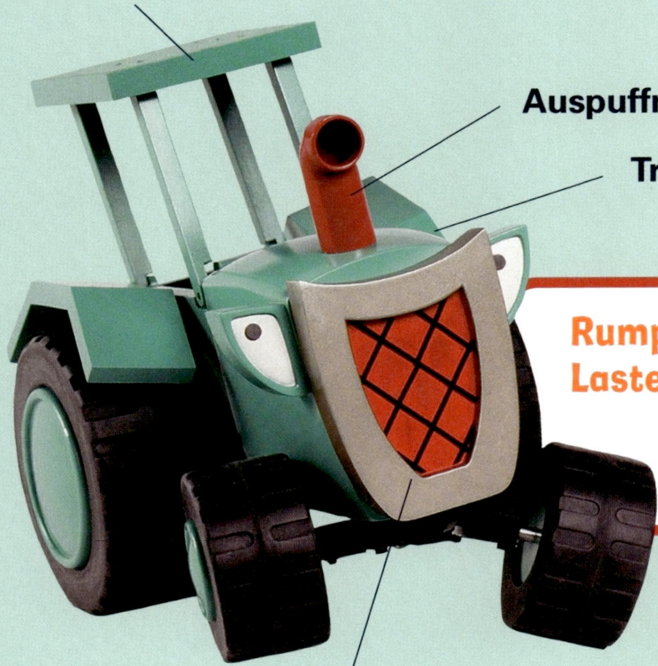

Rumpel, der Trecker, ist mein Name;
Lasten zu transportieren ist mein Job!
Rumpel tractor is my name,
moving loads is my game.

Hallo, ich heiße Baggi!
Hello, my name is Baggi!

Können wir das transportieren?
Can we move it?

Kein Problem!
No problem!

OK, es kann losgehen!
OK, ready to go!

Das Team – The Team

Knolle ist zur Stelle!
Knolle is in charge!
Ich bin gekommen, um zu helfen!
I've come to lend a hand!
Ich bin in allem der Beste!
I'm the best at everything!

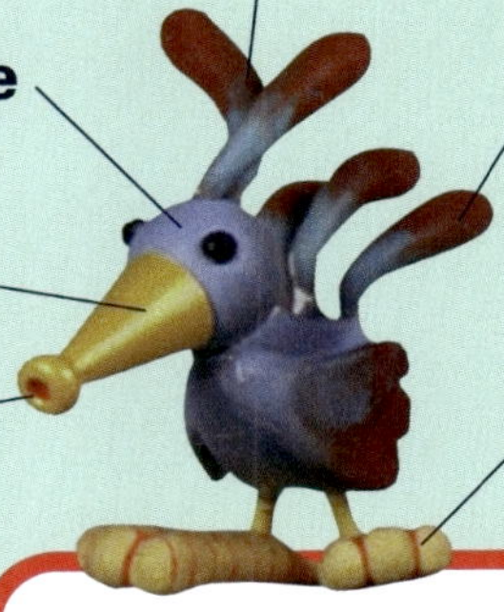

Das ist Feder!
This is Feder!

Knolle unterhält sich mit Feder.
Knolle is talking to Feder.

Das Team – The Team

Das ist eine Katze! This is a cat!

Sie heißt Kuschel. Her name is Kuschel.

Kuschel wartet auf ihr Futter.
Sie hat Hunger!
Kuschel is waiting for her food.
She is hungry!

Kuschel mag Finn, den Fisch!
Kuschel likes Finn the fish!

Das ist ein Hund! This is a dog!

Er heißt Bello. His name is Bello.

Bello schnüffelt an seinem Knochen.
Bello is sniffing at his bone.

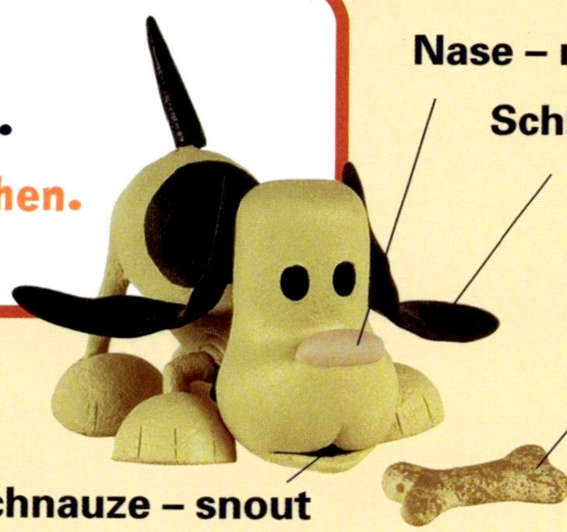

Bauer Gurke geht mit Bello spazieren.
Farmer Gurke is going for a walk with Bello.

Das Team – The Team

Bob und sein Team hoffen, dass du viel Spaß beim Englischlernen hast!
Bob and his team hope you have a lot of fun learning English!

Was braucht Bob bei seiner Arbeit?
What does Bob need for his work?

Was braucht Bob bei seiner Arbeit?
Streiche durch, was nicht dazugehört!
What does Bob need for his work?
Cross out the things that do not match.

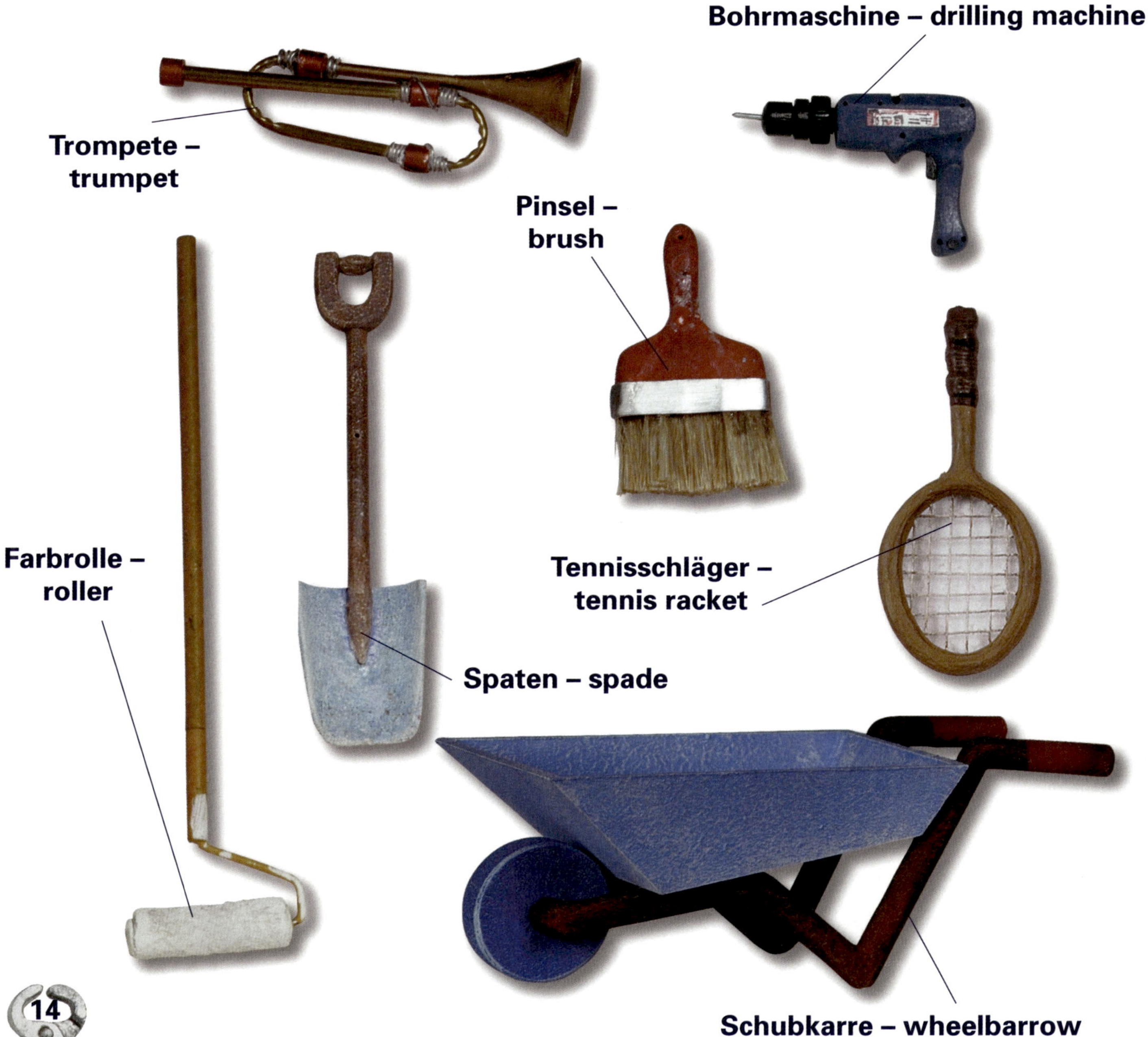

Was braucht Bob bei seiner Arbeit?
What does Bob need for his work?

Bob und Wendy im Wohnzimmer
Bob and Wendy in the living room

Bob und Wendy arbeiten im Wohnzimmer von Frau Breitenbach.

Bob and Wendy are working in Mrs. Breitenbach's living room.

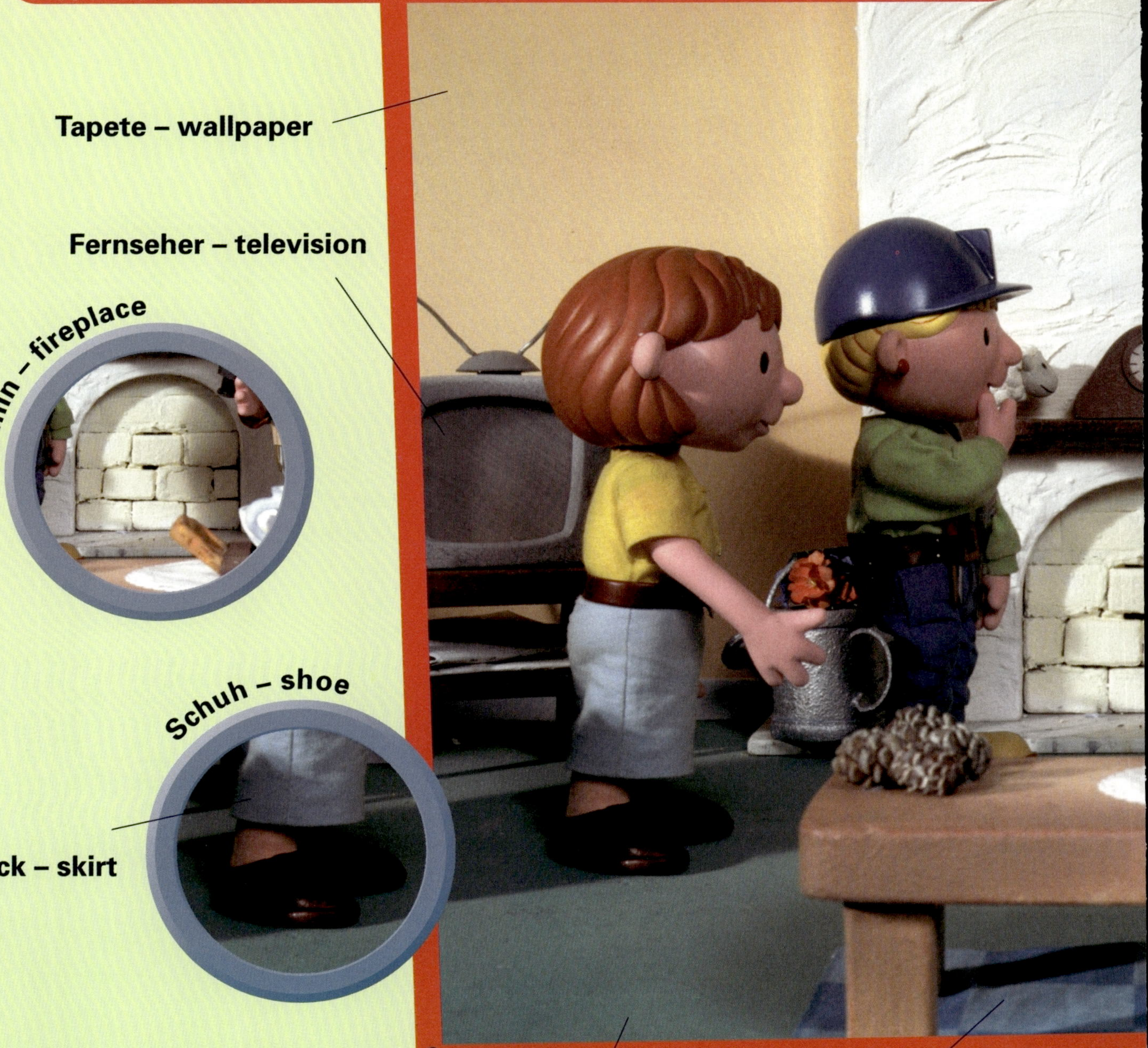

Bob und Wendy im Wohnzimmer
Bob and Wendy in the living room

Was machst du, Bob?
What are you doing, Bob?

Bob isst.
Bob is eating.

Bob hämmert.
Bob is hammering.

Bob sägt Holz.
Bob is sawing wood.

Bob harkt.
Bob is raking.

Bob ruft Wendy an.
Bob is calling Wendy.

Was machst du, Bob?
What are you doing, Bob?

Bob macht eine Pause.
Bob is having a break.

Bob steht auf einer Leiter.
Bob is standing on a ladder.

Bob fährt mit Rollo zur Arbeit.
Bob is driving to work with Rollo.

Bob schiebt eine Schubkarre voller Ziegelsteine.
Bob is pushing a wheel-barrow full of bricks.

Bob versucht zu tapezieren.
Bob is trying to wallpaper.

Knolle zählt gerne
Knolle likes counting

Knolle zählt gerne. Hilfst du ihm?
Knolle likes counting.
Will you help him?

1 eins – one

2 zwei – two

3 drei – three

4 vier – four

5 fünf – five

6 sechs – six

7 sieben – seven

8 acht – eight

9 neun – nine

10 zehn – ten

Knolle zählt gerne
Knolle likes counting

Zähle die folgenden Gegenstände in den Bildern!
Count the following things in the pictures!

Wie viele Ziegelsteine kannst du in diesem Bild finden?
How many bricks can you find in this picture?

Lösung: 8

Wie viele Igel siehst du?
How many hedgehogs do you see?

Lösung: 4

Wie viele Wolken siehst du am Himmel?
How many clouds do you see in the sky?

Lösung: 3

Wie viele Hamster sitzen im Käfig?
How many hamsters are sitting in the cage?

Lösung: 2

Wie viele Geschenke hat Bob bekommen?
How many presents has Bob got?

Lösung: 6

Wie viele Hasen spielen auf der Wiese?
How many rabbits are playing on the meadow?

Lösung: 5

Finde zehn Unterschiede
Find ten differences

Finde die 10 Unterschiede im rechten Bild.
Find the 10 differences in the picture on the right.

Finde zehn Unterschiede
Find ten differences

Lösung:

Bob in der Küche
Bob in the kitchen

Bob arbeitet in der Küche.
Bob is working in the kitchen.

Schrank – cupboard

Wasserkocher – kettle

Daumen – thumb

Stichsäge – jigsaw

Kabel – wire

Bob in der Küche
Bob in the kitchen

Was machst du, Wendy?
What are you doing, Wendy?

Wendy füttert Kuschel.
Wendy is feeding Kuschel.

Wendy sucht im Werkzeugkasten nach einer Zange.
Wendy is searching for the wrench in the toolbox.

Wendy schaut sich im Spiegel an.
Wendy is looking at herself in the mirror.

Wendy trägt einen Regenmantel.
Wendy is wearing a raincoat.

Wendy hat ein Geschenk bekommen.
Wendy has got a present.

Was machst du, Wendy?
What are you doing, Wendy?

Wendy hält einen Teddy in ihren Armen.
Wendy is holding a teddy in her arms.

Wendy spielt Golf.
Wendy is playing golf.

Wendy liest Kuschel eine Geschichte vor.
Wendy is reading a story to Kuschel.

Wendy fährt mit Heppo zur Arbeit.
Wendy is driving to work with Heppo.

Bob und Wendy bauen eine Mauer.
Bob and Wendy are building a wall.

Wie fühlst du dich?
How do you feel?

Knolle ist vergnügt!
Knolle is cheerful!

Wendy ist nachdenklich.
Wendy is thoughtful.

Mixi ist fröhlich.
Mixi is happy.

Heppo ist ängstlich.
Heppo is frightened.

Kuschel ist neugierig.
Kuschel is curious.

Bello ist erstaunt.
Bello is astonished.

Wie fühlst du dich?
How do you feel?

**Wie siehst du aus,
wenn du fröhlich bist?
Male es hier auf!**
**What do you look like
when you're happy?
Draw a picture here!**

**Wie siehst du aus,
wenn du wütend bist?
Male es hier auf!**
**What do you look like
when you're angry?
Draw a picture here!**

Was ist dein Hobby?
What is your hobby?

Bob macht gerne Sport.
Bob likes doing sports.

Mixi hört gerne Popmusik.
Mixi likes listening to pop music.

Mixi, Bello und Kuschel spielen gerne Fußball.
Mixi, Bello and Kuschel like playing football.

Bauer Gurke geht gerne mit Bello spazieren.
Farmer Gurke likes going for a walk with Bello.

Knolle tanzt gerne.
Knolle likes dancing.

Was ist dein Hobby?
What is your hobby?

Feder singt gerne.
Feder likes singing.

Wendy spielt gerne Tennis.
Wendy likes playing tennis.

Und was ist dein Hobby?
And what is your hobby?

Du kannst dein Hobby hier aufmalen oder aufschreiben:
You can draw or write your hobby down here:

Suche, finde und verbinde
Search, find and connect

Verbinde jedes Bild mit dem passenden englischen Wort.
Connect each picture with the correct English word.

Fußball

Eimer

Hamster

Banane

Kuchen

Maus

Schildkröte

Geschenk

Tasse

Eier

Ampel

Computer

Leiter

Fernglas

- football
- banana
- pie
- bucket
- mouse
- hamster
- present
- ladder
- tortoise
- traffic light
- binoculars
- eggs
- cup
- computer

Suche, finde und verbinde
Search, find and connect

Buddel, Rollo und Baggi erledigen heute unterschiedliche Jobs. Wohin fahren sie? Wenn du die Linien verfolgst, kannst du es herausfinden!

Buddel, Rollo and Baggi are doing different jobs today. Where are they driving? If you follow the lines, you will find out!

Ein Tag mit Bob
A day with Bob

Guten Morgen! Bob und Wendy bereiten sich im Büro auf den Tag vor.

Good morning! Bob and Wendy are getting prepared for the day in the office.

Bob und sein Team sind auf ihrem Weg zur Arbeit.

Bob and his team are on their way to work.

Alle arbeiten fleißig.

Everybody is working hard.

Bob und Knolle machen eine Pause.

Bob and Knolle are having a break.

Ein Tag mit Bob
A day with Bob

Nach dem Mittagessen repariert Bob das Dach.
After lunch Bob is repairing the roof.

Heppo ist glücklich, dass er Bob helfen kann.
Heppo is happy to help Bob.

Bob und Wendy machen Feierabend und gehen nach Hause.
Bob and Wendy finish work and go home.

Zähle Schäfchen mit Knolle. Gute Nacht! Schlaf schön!
Count the sheep with Knolle. Good night! Sleep well!

Bob im Badezimmer
Bob in the bathroom

Nach einem langen Tag geht Bob am Abend in die Badewanne! Das wird ein Spaß!
After a long day Bob is taking a bath in the evening. That will be fun!

Spiegel – mirror

Zahnbürste – toothbrush

Zahnpasta – toothpaste

Waschbecken – wash basin

Wasserhahn – tap

Badelatschen – flip flops

Badematte – bathmat

Bob im Badezimmer
Bob in the bathroom

Wo bist du?
Where are you?

Bob steht auf der Leiter.
Bob is standing on the ladder.

Kuschel und Bello stehen neben dem Schild.
Kuschel and Bello are standing next to the sign.

Wendy steht vor dem Spiegel.
Wendy is standing in front of the mirror.

Knolle lehnt sich an den Zaun.
Knolle is leaning on the fence.

Wo bist du?
Where are you?

Kuschel versteckt sich zwischen den Ostereiern.
Kuschel is hiding between the easter eggs.

Heppo steht unter der Brücke.
Heppo is standing under the bridge.

Wendy und Bob stehen hinter der Mauer.
Wendy and Bob are standing behind the wall.

Kannst du die Wolken über Bobs Hof sehen?
Can you see the clouds above Bob's yard?

Fotos – Photos

Der Bürgermeister hat ein paar Fotos gemacht!
The mayor has taken a few photos!
Kannst du die Bildausschnitte den richtigen Fotos zuordnen?
Can you assign the cuttings to the right photos?

Wendy arbeitet in ihrem Büro.
Wendy is working in her office.

1

2

Knolle spielt mit dem Flugzeug.
Knolle is playing with the aeroplane.

4

3

Kuschel fühlt sich sehr wohl in Bobs Sessel.
Kuschel is feeling very comfortable in Bob's armchair.

Bob hat Post bekommen!
Bob has got mail!

Knolle hat einen Schneemann gebaut.
Knolle has built a snowman.

5

Fotos – Photos

A

B

C

D

E

Hier kannst du dein Lieblingsfoto einkleben!
You can stick your favourite photo here!

Lösung: 1=E; 2=D; 3=A; 4=C; 5=B

Armer Heppo! – Poor Heppo!

Alle Tiere wollen mit Heppo spielen.
All animals want to play with Heppo.

Nach der Arbeit – After work

Bob und Wendy sind mit ihren Freunden zum Abendessen in einem Restaurant.

Bob and Wendy are having dinner with their friends in a restaurant.

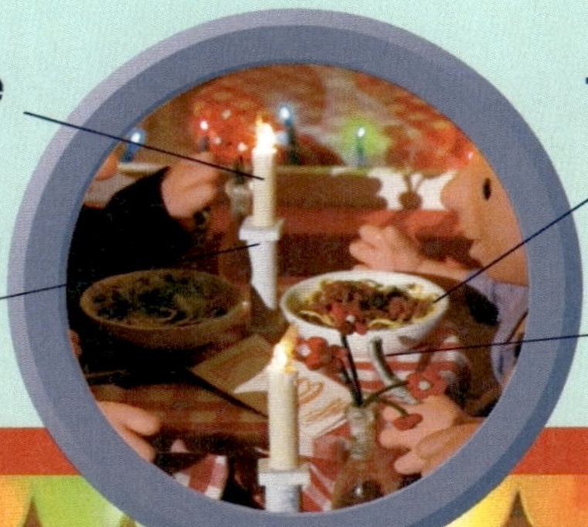

Wörterverzeichnis – Vocabulary list

A
Abend – evening [ˈiːvnɪŋ]
Abendessen – dinner [ˈdɪnə(r)]
acht – eight [eɪt]
Akten – files [faɪlz]
alle – everybody [ˈɛvrɪbodɪ]
alles – everything [ˈɛvrɪθɪŋ]
Ampel – traffic light [ˈtræfɪk ˈlaɪt]
an – at/to [æt]; [tuː]
anfangen – (to) start [tuː ˈstɒrt]
ängstlich – frightened [ˈfraɪtənd]
anhören – (to) listen [tuː ˈlɪsən]
anrufen – (to) call [tuː kɔːl]
anschauen – (to) look at [tuː luk æt]
Anzug – suit [suːt]
Arbeit – work [wɜːk]
arbeiten – (to) work [tuː wɜːk]
Arm – arm [ɒrm]
arm – poor [por]
auf – on [ɒn]
Auge – eye [ɑɪ]
Auspuffrohr – exhaust pipe [ˈɪgˈzɔːst ˈpaɪp]
aussehen – (to) look [tuː lʊk]
B
Badelatschen – flip flops [ˈflɪpˈflɒps]
Badematte – bathmat [ˈbɑːθmæt]
Badewanne – bathtub [ˈbɑːθˈtʌb]
Badezimmer – bathroom [ˈbɑːθruːm]
Banane – banana [bəˈnaːnə]
Bauer – farmer [ˈfɒrmə(r)]
bauen – (to) build [tuː bɪld]
Baugeschäft – building yard [ˈbɪldɪŋ ˈyɒrd]
Baum – tree [trɪː]
Baumeister – builder [ˈbɪldə(r)]
Bein – leg [leg]
bekommen – (to) get [tuː get]
Beste(r) – best [best]
Beton – concrete [ˈkoŋkriːt]
Bild – picture [ˈpɪktʃə(r)]
Bildschirm – screen [skriːn]
blau – blue [bluː]
Blume – flower [ˈflaʊə(r)]
Blumentopf – flowerpot [ˈflaʊə(r)pɒt]
bohren – (to) drill [tuː drɪl]
Bohrmaschine – drilling machine [ˈdrɪlɪŋ məˈʃiːn]
Brille – glasses [ˈglaːsəz]
Brücke – bridge [brɪdʒ]
Buch – book [bʊk]
Bürgermeister – mayor [ˈmeə(r)]
Büro – office [ˈɒfɪs]
Busch – bush [bʊʃ]
C
Computer – computer [ˈkəmˈpjuːtə(r)]
D
Dach – roof [ruːf]
Dampfwalze – steamroller [ˈstiːmrəolə(r)]
Daumen – thumb [θʌm]
Decke – ceiling [ˈsiːlɪŋ]
drei – three [θriː]
du – you [juː]

E
Ei – egg [eg]
Eichhörnchen – squirrel [ˈskwɪrəl]
Eimer – bucket [ˈbʌkɪt]
eins – one [wʌn]
englisch – English [ˈɪŋglɪʃ]
Ente – duck [dʌk]
erstaunt – astonished [ˈəˈstɒnɪʃt]
essen – (to) eat [tuː iːt]
F
fahren – (to) drive [tuː draɪv]
Farbrolle – roller [ˈrəʊlə(r)]
Feder – feather [ˈfɛðə(r)]
Fehler – mistake [ˈmɪsteɪk]
Fell – fur [fɜː]
Fenster – window [ˈwɪndəʊ]
Fensterbank – window sill [ˈwɪndəʊ ˈsɪl]
Fernglas – binoculars [baɪˈnəkjuləz]
Fernseher – television [ˈtelɪvɪʒən]
Finger – finger [ˈfɪŋgə(r)]
finden – (to) find [tuː faɪnd]
Fisch – fish [fiʃ]
fleißig – diligent [ˈdɪlɪdʒənt]
Flugzeug – aeroplane [ˈeərəʊpleɪn]
folgen – (to) follow [tuː ˈfɒləʊ]
Foto – photo [ˈfəʊtəʊ]
Freund – friend [frend]
fröhlich – happy [ˈhæpɪ]
fühlen – (to) feel [tuː fiːl]
fünf – five [faɪv]
füttern – (to) feed [tuː fiːd]
Fuß – foot [fʊt]
Fußball – football [ˈfʊtbɔːl]
Fußboden – floor [flɔːr]
Futter – food [fuːd]
G
Gabel – fork [fɔːrk]
Gardine – curtain [ˈkɜːtən]
Gegenstand – thing [θɪŋ]
gehen – (to) go [tuː gəʊ]
gelb – yellow [ˈjeləʊ]
gerne haben/mögen – (to) like [tuː laɪk]
Geschenk – present [ˈprezənt]
Geschichte – story [ˈstɔːri]
Glas – glass [glaːs]
glücklich – happy [ˈhæpɪ]
Golf – golf [gɒlf]
groß – big [bɪg]
grün – green [griːn]
Gürtel – belt [belt]
gut – good [gʊd]
H
Haar – hair [heə(r)]
haben – (to) have [tuː hæv]
Hahn – cock [kɒk]
Haken – hook [hʊk]
halten – (to) hold [tuː həuld]
hämmern – (to) hammer [tuː ˈhæmə(r)]
hallo – hello [ˈhəˈləʊ]
Hamster – hamster [ˈhæmstə(r)]

Wörterverzeichnis – Vocabulary list

Hand – hand [hænd]
Handtuch – towel [ˈtaʊəl]
harken – (to) rake [tuː reɪk]
Hase – hare [heə(r)]
Haus – house [haʊs]
helfen – (to) help [tuː help]
Helm – helmet [ˈhelmət]
Hemd – shirt [ʃɜːt]
heute – today [təˈdeɪ]
hier – here [hɪr]
Himmel – sky [skaɪ]
hinter – behind [bɪˈhaɪnd]
Hobby – hobby [ˈhɒbɪ]
hochheben – (to) lift [tuː lɪft]
hoffen – (to) hope [tuː həup]
hören – (to) hear [tuː hɪr]
Hof – yard [jaːd]
Holz – wood [wʊd]
Hose – trousers [ˈtraʊzəz]
Huhn – chicken [ˈtʃɪkɪn]
Hund – dog [dɒg]
Hunger – hunger [ˈhʌŋgə(r)]
Hut – hat [hæt]
I
ich – I [aɪ]
Igel – hedgehog [ˈhɛdʒhʊg]
in/im – in [ɪn]
J
Jalousie – venetian blind [vəˈniːʃən ˈblaɪnd]
Jeans – jeans [dʒiːnz]
Job – job [dʒɒb]
K
Kabel – wire [ˈwaɪə(r)]
Kachel – tile [taɪl]
Käfig – cage [keɪdʒ]
Kaffeemaschine – coffee machine [ˈkɒfɪ məˈʃiːn]
Kamin – fireplace [ˈfaɪə(r)pleɪs]
Kaninchen – rabbit [ˈræbɪt]
Katze – cat [kæt]
Kellner – waiter [ˈweɪtə(r)]
Kerze – candle [ˈkændl]
Kerzenständer – candlestick [ˈkændlstɪk]
Kipper – dump truck [ˈdʌmp ˈtrʌk]
Knochen – bone [bəʊn]
können – (to) can [tuː kæn]
Kopf – head [hed]
Krähe – crow [krəʊ]
Kralle – talon [tælən]
Kran – crane [kreɪn]
Krawatte – tie [taɪ]
Kuchen – pie [paɪ]
Küche – kitchen [ˈkɪtʃɪn]
Kühlergrill – radiator grill [ˈreɪdɪeɪtə(r) grɪl]
L
Lächeln – smile [smaɪl]
Lampe – lamp [læmp]
lang – long [lɒːŋ]
Latzhose – overall [ˈəʊvˈrɔːl]
lehnen – (to) lean [tuː liːn]
Leiter – ladder [ˈlædə(r)]
Leine – leash [liːʃ]
lernen – (to) learn [tuː lɜːn]
lesen – (to) read [tuː rɪːd]
Linie – line [laɪn]
Loch – hole [həʊl]
Lumpen – rags [rægz]
M
machen – (to) do [tuː duː]
malen – (to) draw [tuː drɔː]
Mauer – wall [wɔːl]
Maus – mouse [maʊs]
mischen – (to) mix [tuː mɪks]
mit – with [wɪθ]
Mittagessen – lunch [lʌntʃ]
Morgen – morning [ˈmɔːrnɪŋ]
Mund – mouth [maʊθ]
N
nach – after [ˈaːftə(r)]
nachdenklich – thoughtful [ˈθɔːtfəl]
Nacht – night [nəɪt]
Name – name [neɪm]
Napf – bowl [bəʊl]
Nase – nose [nəʊs]
neben – next to [nekst tuː]
neugierig – curious [ˈkjʊarɪəs]
neun – nine [naɪn]
O
Ohr – ear [ɪə(r)]
Ohrring – earring [ˈɪərɪŋ]
orange – orange [ˈɒrɪndʒ]
Osterei – easter egg [ˈiːstər eg]
P
Pause – break [breɪk]
Pferdeschwanz – ponytail [ˈpəʊnɪteɪl]
Pfote – paw [pɔː]
Pinnwand – pinboard [ˈpɪnbɔːd]
Pinsel – brush [brʌʃ]
Popmusik – pop music [ˈpɒpˈmjuːzɪk]
Post – mail [meɪl]
Problem – problem [ˈprɒbləm]
Pullover – pullover [ˈpuləʊvə(r)]
R
Rad – wheel [wiːl]
Raupenkette – caterpillar [ˈkætəpɪlə(r)]
rechts – right [raɪt]
Regal – shelf [ʃelf]
Regenmantel – raincoat [ˈreɪnkəʊt]
Reifen – tyre [taɪə(r)]
reparieren – (to) repair [tuː rɪˈpɛə(r)]
Restaurant – restaurant [ˈrɛstarɒnt]
richtig – right [raɪt]
Rock – skirt [skɜːt]
rot – red [red]
Rübe – beet [biːt]
S
Säge – saw [sɔː]
sägen – (to) saw [tuː sɔː]
Sägespäne – shavings [ˈʃeɪvɪŋz]
Schaf – sheep [ʃiːp]
Schal – scarf [skɒːf]

Wörterverzeichnis – Vocabulary list

Schaufel – shovel [ˈʃʌvl]
Schild – sign [saɪn]
Schildkröte – tortoise [ˈtɔːtəs]
schlafen – (to) sleep [tuː sliːp]
Schlappohr – ear [ɪə(r)]
Schnabel – beak [biːk]
Schnauze – snout [snaʊt]
Schneemann – snowman [ˈsnəʊmæn]
Schneepflug – snowplough [ˈsnəʊplaʊ]
Schnurrbart – moustache [məˈstaːʃ]
Schnurrhaare – whiskers [ˈwɪskəz]
Schornstein – chimney [ˈtʃɪmnɪ]
Schrank – cupboard [ˈkʌbəːd]
Schraubenschlüssel – wrench [rɛntʃ]
Schraubenzieher – screwdriver [ˈskruːdraɪvə(r)]
Schraubzwinge – screw clamp [ˈskruː klæmp]
schreiben – (to) write [tuː raɪt]
Schreibtisch – desk [desk]
Schubkarre – wheelbarrow [ˈwiːlbærəʊ]
Schuh – shoe [ʃuː]
Schutzbrille – safety goggles [ˈseɪfti ˈgɒglz]
Schwamm – sponge [spʌndʒ]
Schwanz – tail [teɪl]
sechs – six [sɪks]
sehen – (to) see [tuː siː]
Sessel – armchair [ˈaːmˈtʃeə(r)]
sieben – seven [ˈsevn]
singen – (to) sing [tuː sɪŋ]
sitzen – (to) sit [tuː sɪt]
Sofa – sofa [ˈsəʊfə]
Spachtel – spatula [ˈspætjələ]
Spaß – fun [fʌn]
Spaten – spade [speɪd]
Speisekarte – menu [ˈmenjuː]
Spiegel – mirror [ˈmɪrə(r)]
spielen – (to) play [tuː pleɪ]
Spitzhacke – pickaxe [ˈpɪkæks]
Sport – sport [spɔːrt]
stehen – (to) stand [tuː stænd]
Stichsäge – jigsaw [ˈdʒɪgsɔː]
Stiefel – boots [buːts]
Streifen – stripe [straɪp]
Stuhl – chair [tʃeə(r)]
suchen – (to) search [tuː sɜːtʃ]

T

Tablett – tray [treɪ]
Tag – day [deɪ]
tanzen – (to) dance [tuː daːns]
Tapete – wallpaper [ˈwɔːlpeɪpə(r)]
tapezieren – (to) wallpaper [tuːˈwɔːlpeɪpə(r)]
Tasse – cup [kʌp]
Team – team [tiːm]
Teddy – teddy [ˈtedɪː]
Teekanne – teapot [ˈtiːpɒt]
Telefon – telephone [ˈtelɪfəʊn]
Teller – plate [pleɪt]
Tennis – tennis [ˈtenɪs]
Tennisschläger – tennis racket [ˈtenɪsˈrækɪt]
Teppich – carpet [ˈkaːpɪt]
Terrasse – terrace [ˈterɪs]
Tier – animal [ˈænɪməl]
Tisch – table [ˈteɪbl]
Tischdecke – tablecloth [ˈteɪblklɒːθ]
Toast – toast [təʊst]
Traktor – tractor [ˈtræktə(r)]
Trompete – trumpet [ˈtrʌmpɪt]
Tür – door [dɔːr]
Türknauf – doorknob [dɔːrnɒb]

U

über – above [ˈəbʌv]
Uhr – clock [klɒk]
und – and [ænd]
unter – under [ˈʌndə(r)]
unterhalten – (to) talk [tuː tɔːk]

V

verbinden – (to) connect [tuː kəˈnekt]
vergnügt – cheerful [ˈtʃɪəfəl]
verschieben – (to) shift [tuː ʃɪft]
verstecken – (to) hide [tuː haɪd]
vier – four [fɔːr]
Vogel – bird [bɜːd]
Vogelscheuche – scarecrow [ˈskeəkrəʊ]
vor – in front of [ɪnˈfrʌnt əv]
vorbereiten – (to) prepare [tuː prɪˈpea(r)]

W

Warnsignal – warning signal [ˈwɔːnɪŋ ˈsɪgnəl]
warten – (to) wait [tuː weɪt]
Waschbecken – wash basin [ˈwɒʃˈbeɪsən]
Wasser – water [ˈwɔːtə(r)]
Wasserhahn – tap [tæp]
Wasserkocher – kettle [ˈketl]
Weg – way [weɪ]
wenn – if [ɪf]
Werkstatt – workshop [ˈwɔːkʃɒp]
Werkzeugkasten – toolbox [ˈtuːlbɒks]
Weste – waistcoat [ˈweɪstkəʊt]
Wiese – meadow [ˈmedəʊ]
wo – where [(h)weə(r)]
Wohnzimmer – living room [ˈlɪvɪŋˈruːm]
Wolke – cloud [klaʊd]
Wort – word [wɜːd]
wütend – angry [æŋgri]

Z

zählen – (to) count [tuː kaʊnt]
Zahnbürste – toothbrush [ˈtuːθbrʌʃ]
Zahnpasta – toothpaste [ˈtuːθpeɪst]
Zange – pliers [plaɪəz]
Zaun – fence [fens]
zehn – ten [ten]
Zement – cement [sɪˈment]
Zettel – piece of paper [piːs ˈəʌ ˈpeɪpə(r)]
Ziegelstein – brick [brɪk]
Zunge – tongue [tʌŋ]
zusammen – together [təˈgɛðə(r)]
zwei – two [tuː]

Memory – Memory

Schneide die Spielkarten aus. Vermische sie und verteile sie dann mit den Bildern nach unten auf dem Tisch. Immer zwei Karten gehören zusammen. Kannst du sie finden?

Baum

tree

Schild

sign

Krähe

crow

Schildkröte

tortoise

Eimer

bucket

Kuchen

pie

Pinsel

brush

Trompete

trumpet

Blumentopf

flowerpot

Geschenk

present

Memory – Memory

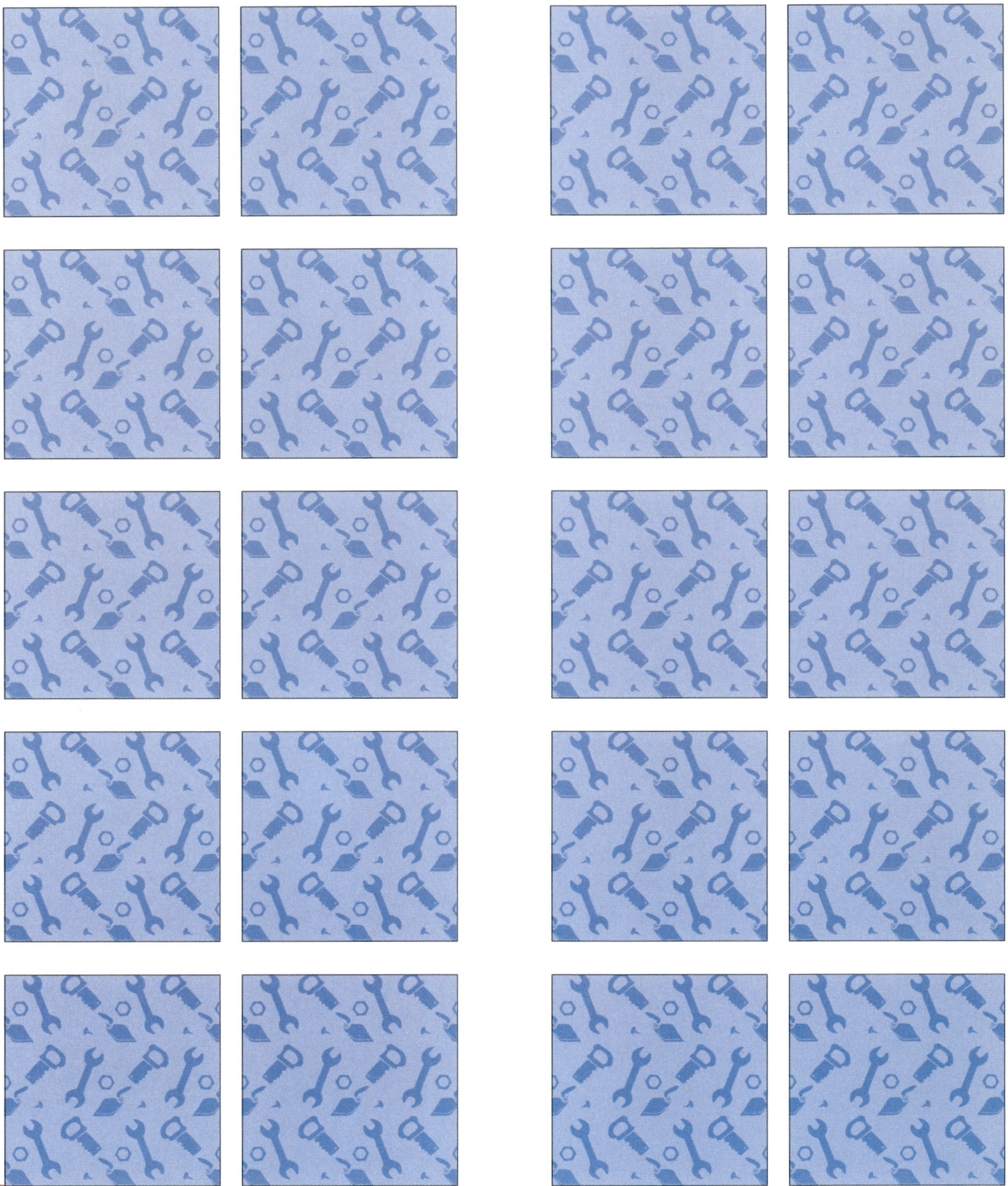